The Power of Focus

Mastering Productivity, Reducing Stress, and Achieving Success Through Mindfulness Practices

Mindfulness Techniques For Young Professionals And Entrepreneurs

ASPM

Table of Contents

Chapter 1

Introduction to Focus and Mindfulness

The Importance of Focus in Today's Fast-Paced World

In today's fast-paced world, where distractions are abundant and the pace of life accelerates daily, the importance of focus cannot be overstated. Young professionals, entrepreneurs, students, and anyone striving for personal growth must recognize that the ability to concentrate deeply on tasks is not just advantageous but essential for success. The modern environment, characterized by constant notifications, multitasking demands, and information overload, can easily derail even the most determined individuals from their goals. Cultivating focus, therefore, becomes a fundamental skill that can significantly enhance performance across various domains, including career advancement, academic achievement, and personal development.

The brain's plasticity plays a pivotal role in shaping our ability to concentrate. Neuroplasticity, the brain's capacity to reorganize itself by forming new neural connections, means that individuals can train their brains to enhance focus and cognitive function. Engaging in mindfulness practices, for instance, has been shown to strengthen the areas of the brain responsible for attention and emotional regulation. By incorporating techniques such as meditation and focused breathing into daily routines, young professionals and entrepreneurs can improve their mental clarity, reduce stress, and enhance their decision-making skills. This training fosters resilience, enabling individuals to navigate challenges more effectively and maintain their focus under pressure.

Moreover, the relationship between nutrition and cognitive performance underscores the importance of a well-rounded approach to enhancing focus. Certain dietary choices can significantly impact brain health and function. Foods rich in omega-3 fatty acids, antioxidants, and vitamins can help optimize cognitive abilities. Young professionals and students, in particular, should prioritize nutrition to fuel their brains, ensuring they possess the mental acuity needed for high-stakes environments. By adopting a diet that supports cognitive function, individuals can improve their concentration, memory, and overall productivity, thus positioning themselves for greater success in their endeavors.

Physical exercise also plays a critical role in enhancing focus and mental well-being. Regular physical activity increases blood flow to the brain, promoting the growth of new neurons and improving synaptic plasticity. Athletes and professionals alike can benefit from integrating various forms of exercise into their routines, as physical conditioning not only boosts physical health but also sharpens mental faculties. The interplay between physical activity and cognitive performance highlights the importance of maintaining a balanced lifestyle that prioritizes both mental and physical health for optimal focus and productivity.

Lastly, effective time management strategies are essential for cultivating focus in a world rife with distractions. Establishing productive habits and routines can significantly reduce overwhelm and increase efficiency. Techniques such as the Pomodoro Technique, which encourages structured periods of focused work followed by short breaks, can help individuals maintain their concentration over longer periods. Additionally, understanding the impact of quality sleep on cognitive function is crucial; poor sleep can diminish focus, decision- making abilities, and overall performance. By prioritizing sleep hygiene and managing time wisely, professionals and students can enhance their focus, set actionable goals, and achieve the success they aspire to.

Understanding Mindfulness: Definition and Benefits

Mindfulness, often defined as the practice of being fully present and engaged in the moment without judgment, has garnered significant attention for its potential benefits across various aspects of life. At its core, mindfulness encourages individuals to cultivate awareness of their thoughts, feelings, and surroundings, fostering a deeper connection with themselves and their environment. This state of awareness allows for improved focus, reduced stress, and enhanced emotional regulation, making it an invaluable tool for young professionals, entrepreneurs, students, and anyone seeking to enhance their cognitive abilities and personal growth.

The benefits of mindfulness extend far beyond mere relaxation techniques. Research has demonstrated that regular mindfulness practice can lead to significant improvements in cognitive function, such as heightened concentration, better memory retention, and improved decision-making skills. For young professionals and entrepreneurs, these cognitive enhancements are crucial for navigating the complexities of the workplace and making strategic decisions that can impact their careers. Furthermore, students can experience better academic performance and reduced exam anxiety through mindfulness, allowing them to approach their studies with clarity and focus.

In addition to cognitive improvements, mindfulness is linked to emotional intelligence development. By fostering greater self-awareness and emotional regulation, individuals can improve their interpersonal relationships and leadership skills. This is particularly relevant for executives and managers, who must navigate team dynamics and foster a positive work environment. Mindfulness training encourages leaders to respond thoughtfully rather than react impulsively, promoting a culture of empathy and understanding within their organizations. As a result, both personal and professional relationships can benefit significantly from the cultivation of mindfulness.

Another important aspect of mindfulness is its role in stress reduction. The fast-paced nature of modern life can lead to overwhelming feelings, which can diminish productivity and overall well- being. Mindfulness practices help individuals recognize stress triggers and develop healthier coping mechanisms. By integrating mindfulness into their daily routines, professionals, athletes, and personal development enthusiasts can enhance their resilience and maintain a balanced approach to challenges. This not only boosts mental clarity but also contributes to overall mental health and well-being.

Ultimately, understanding mindfulness and its myriad benefits equips individuals with the tools necessary to thrive in their personal and professional lives. By embracing mindfulness techniques, one can unlock the brain's potential for neuroplasticity, reinforcing positive habits and behaviors that lead to success. In a world where distractions abound and demands are high, cultivating mindfulness offers a pathway to greater focus, improved cognitive performance, and a more fulfilling life. Whether you are a young professional starting your career, an entrepreneur navigating the business landscape, or simply someone looking to optimize your mental capabilities, mindfulness can serve as a powerful ally in your journey toward success.

Overview of Techniques to Enhance Focus

In today's fast-paced world, the ability to focus effectively is more crucial than ever, especially for young professionals, entrepreneurs, and students. This chapter provides an overview of techniques designed to enhance focus, drawing on principles from mindfulness, neuroplasticity, and cognitive behavioral strategies. By understanding and implementing these techniques, individuals can train their brains to achieve greater success, whether in the workplace, academic settings, or personal endeavors.

One of the most effective ways to enhance focus is through mindfulness and meditation practices. These techniques encourage individuals to cultivate present-moment awareness, which can significantly reduce distractions and stress. Regular mindfulness exercises, such as deep breathing and guided meditations, have been shown to improve cognitive function by promoting relaxation and clarity of thought. Young professionals and students alike can benefit from incorporating these practices into their daily routines, as they not only foster concentration but also enhance emotional regulation and resilience under pressure.

Neuroplasticity techniques offer another powerful avenue for enhancing focus. The brain's remarkable ability to reorganize itself means that individuals can actively reshape their cognitive pathways to improve performance and mental acuity. Engaging in activities that challenge the brain-such as learning new skills, solving puzzles, or practicing memory enhancement techniques-can lead to increased focus and cognitive flexibility. This is particularly relevant for entrepreneurs and executives who need to adapt quickly to changing environments and make strategic decisions efficiently.

Nutrition also plays a vital role in cognitive performance and focus. Research has demonstrated that a well-balanced diet rich in essential nutrients supports brain health, leading to improved mental clarity and productivity. Specific foods, such as fatty fish, nuts, and leafy greens, are known for their brain-boosting properties. Young professionals and students should pay attention to their dietary choices, as optimizing nutrition can enhance their ability to concentrate and perform at their best, especially during high-stakes situations like exams or business negotiations.

Physical exercise is another key component in the quest for enhanced focus. Regular physical activity has been linked to increased blood flow to the brain, promoting the growth of new neurons and improving overall cognitive function. Whether through aerobic exercises, strength training, or even mindfulness-based activities like yoga, incorporating movement into one's routine can lead to better focus and mental clarity. For athletes and professionals alike, understanding the connection between physical health and cognitive performance is essential for achieving peak results in both physical and mental pursuits.

By exploring these diverse techniques- mindfulness practices, neuroplasticity strategies, nutritional optimization, and physical exercise- individuals can develop a comprehensive approach to enhancing focus. Each technique offers unique benefits that collectively contribute to improved cognitive abilities, setting the stage for success in personal and professional endeavors. Embracing these methods is not just about immediate gains; it is about cultivating long-term habits that promote sustained focus and resilience in an increasingly demanding world.

Chapter 2

Neuroplasticity and Personal Growth

The Science of Neuroplasticity

Neuroplasticity, often described as the brain's remarkable ability to reorganize itself by forming new neural connections throughout life, plays a crucial role in personal and professional development. This scientific phenomenon enables the brain to adapt to new experiences, learn new information, and recover from injuries. For young professionals and entrepreneurs, understanding neuroplasticity can unlock powerful strategies for enhancing focus, decision-making, and overall cognitive function. By embracing the principles of neuroplasticity, individuals can cultivate a mindset geared toward continuous growth and improvement.

At its core, neuroplasticity involves the brain's ability to change in response to learning and experience. This process occurs at various levels, from the molecular to the behavioral, allowing individuals to acquire new skills or modify existing ones. For students preparing for exams, this means that implementing effective study techniques can physically alter the brain's structure, enhancing memory retention and recall. Similarly, for executives and managers, fostering an environment that encourages learning and adaptability can lead to improved strategic thinking and innovative problem-solving.

Mindfulness practices, such as meditation and focused breathing exercises, have been shown to promote neuroplasticity. These techniques help to reduce stress and improve cognitive function by enhancing the brain's ability to focus and remain present. By incorporating mindfulness into daily routines, young professionals can train their minds to become more resilient, allowing them to navigate the challenges of their careers with greater ease. Additionally, mindfulness fosters emotional intelligence, enabling individuals to understand and manage their emotions effectively, which is essential for leadership and interpersonal relationships.

Nutrition also plays a significant role in supporting neuroplasticity. The brain requires specific nutrients to function optimally, and a balanced diet rich in antioxidants, healthy fats, vitamins, and minerals can enhance cognitive performance. By prioritizing brain-healthy foods, individuals can improve their mental clarity and focus, providing a solid foundation for personal and professional success. This holistic approach to cognitive enhancement recognizes that both mental and physical well-being are interconnected, and that nurturing the brain through proper nutrition can amplify the benefits of neuroplasticity.

Lastly, physical exercise has been shown to stimulate neuroplasticity, promoting the growth of new neurons and enhancing overall brain function. Engaging in regular physical activity not only boosts mood and energy levels but also sharpens cognitive abilities, making it an essential component of any personal development plan. For athletes and entrepreneurs alike, integrating exercise into daily routines can lead to improved mental acuity and better decision-making. By understanding and leveraging the science of neuroplasticity, individuals can create a powerful framework for personal growth, enabling them to reach their goals and achieve lasting success.

Practical Applications for Young Professionals

Practical applications of mindfulness and focus techniques are essential for young professionals who are navigating the complexities of their early careers. As these individuals strive to build effective habits and develop a mindset that fosters success, they can leverage mindfulness practices to enhance their cognitive abilities. By incorporating techniques such as meditation and focused breathing into their daily routines, young professionals can cultivate mental acuity, reduce stress, and improve decision- making skills. For instance, starting the day with a brief meditation session can help clear the mind and set a positive tone for the challenges ahead, allowing for improved focus during meetings and tasks.

Additionally, understanding the principles of neuroplasticity is crucial for personal growth. Young professionals can harness the brain's remarkable ability to reorganize and adapt by engaging in activities that challenge their cognitive functions. This could include taking on new responsibilities at work, pursuing further education, or even learning a new skill. By stepping outside their comfort zones and continuously stimulating their brains, these individuals can enhance their performance and resilience in the face of adversity, ultimately leading to greater career success.

Nutrition also plays a pivotal role in cognitive performance. Young professionals should be aware of how their dietary choices impact their mental clarity and overall brain health. Incorporating nutrient-dense foods such as leafy greens, fatty fish, and whole grains into their diets can provide essential vitamins and minerals that support cognitive function. Moreover, staying hydrated and avoiding excessive caffeine can further enhance concentration and productivity. By prioritizing nutrition, young professionals can create a solid foundation for optimal mental acuity and sustained focus throughout their workdays.

Physical exercise is another powerful tool for cognitive enhancement. Young professionals can incorporate regular physical activity Into their routines to boost brain function and overall well- being. Activities such as jogging, yoga, or strength training not only promote physical health but also stimulate the release of endorphins and improve mood. Engaging in exercise has been shown to increase neurogenesis-the formation of new neurons-which is vital for maintaining cognitive vitality. By making exercise a priority, young professionals can experience improved focus and energy levels, translating into enhanced productivity and performance at work.

Finally, developing emotional intelligence is crucial for young professionals aiming to build strong interpersonal relationships and effective leadership skills. Techniques such as mindfulness can help individuals become more aware of their emotions and improve their ability to regulate them. This emotional awareness enhances communication skills and fosters empathy, enabling young professionals to navigate workplace dynamics more effectively. By prioritizing emotional intelligence development alongside cognitive strategies, these individuals can create a well-rounded approach to personal and professional growth, ultimately setting themselves up for long-term success in their careers.

Rewiring Your Brain for Success

Rewiring your brain for success is a transformative process that involves understanding and leveraging the principles of neuroplasticity. Neuroplasticity refers to the brain's remarkable ability to reorganize itself by forming new neural connections throughout life. This means that by adopting specific mindsets and habits, young professionals, entrepreneurs, and anyone eager to improve their cognitive function can effectively reshape their brain's wiring to support their goals. Engaging in targeted activities that promote neuroplasticity can enhance mental acuity, creativity, and problem- solving skills, all of which are crucial for success in any field.

One of the most effective ways to harness the power of neuroplasticity is through mindfulness practices. Mindfulness and meditation techniques not only help in reducing stress but also enhance focus and cognitive performance. Regular mindfulness practice encourages individuals to become more aware of their thoughts, emotions, and surroundings, fostering a state of mental clarity that can lead to better decision-making and increased productivity. For young professionals and entrepreneurs, incorporating mindfulness into their daily routines can be a game-changer, allowing them to navigate challenges with a calm and focused mind.

In addition to mindfulness, cognitive behavioral approaches can play a significant role in goal setting and personal development. Utilizing principles from cognitive behavioral therapy (CBT), individuals can identify negative thought patterns and replace them with more constructive beliefs that support their aspirations. This process not only aids in establishing clear, actionable goals but also empowers individuals to develop resilience when faced with setbacks. By rewiring their thought processes, executives, students, and entrepreneurs alike can create a robust framework for achieving their personal and professional objectives.

Nutrition is another critical factor that impacts cognitive performance and brain health. A well- balanced diet rich in essential nutrients can significantly enhance mental clarity and focus. Foods high in omega-3 fatty acids, antioxidants, and vitamins play a vital role in supporting brain function. Young professionals and students should pay attention to their dietary choices, as optimizing nutrition can lead to improved concentration and memory retention. By fueling their bodies with the right nutrients, individuals can create an environment conducive to cognitive enhancement and sustained energy levels.

Lastly, physical exercise has been shown to have profound effects on brain function and overall well-being. Regular physical activity increases blood flow to the brain, promotes the release of neurotrophic factors, and enhances the growth of new neurons. For athletes and busy professionals, integrating various forms of exercise into their routines can serve as a powerful tool for mental conditioning. Whether through aerobic workouts, strength training, or even yoga, the benefits of physical activity extend beyond physical health, contributing significantly to cognitive enhancement and emotional resilience. By adopting a holistic approach that combines mindfulness, nutrition, and physical fitness, individuals can effectively rewire their brains for lasting success.

Chapter 3

Mindfulness Meditation and Practices

Introduction to Mindfulness Techniques

Mindfulness techniques have gained significant recognition in recent years, particularly among young professionals, entrepreneurs, and individuals striving for personal development. As we navigate the complexities of modern life-a fast- paced work environment, academic pressures, and the constant pursuit of success-mindfulness offers a transformative approach to enhancing cognitive abilities and emotional resilience. This subchapter introduces the foundational concepts of mindfulness techniques, focusing on how they can be effectively integrated into daily routines to foster success in various domains.

At its core, mindfulness is the practice of being present and fully engaged in the moment, free from distractions or judgment. This practice not only cultivates awareness but also promotes a deeper understanding of one's thoughts and feelings. For young professionals and entrepreneurs, mastering mindfulness can lead to improved decision-making skills and heightened creativity, essential components of thriving in competitive environments. By training the brain to focus on the present, individuals can reduce the noise of stress and anxiety, creating a mental space conducive to innovative thinking and strategic planning.

The psychological underpinnings of mindfulness are deeply rooted in concepts of neuroplasticity— the brain's ability to reorganize itself by forming new neural connections throughout life. Engaging in mindfulness practices can facilitate this process, enhancing cognitive performance and emotional regulation. As students prepare for exams or young professionals aim to excel in their careers, mindfulness serves as a powerful tool to optimize brain function. Techniques such as meditation, breathing exercises, and mindful observation can sharpen focus, boost memory retention, and improve overall mental clarity, driving success in academic and professional settings.

Moreover, mindfulness techniques extend beyond individual benefits; they also enhance interpersonal relationships and leadership skills. Executives and managers, in particular, can leverage mindfulness to cultivate emotional intelligence, which is integral to effective communication and team dynamics. By fostering a mindful culture within organizations, leaders can promote a positive work environment that encourages collaboration and resilience. This holistic approach not only contributes to personal growth but also drives collective success, showcasing the importance of mindfulness in today's workplace.

Incorporating mindfulness into daily routines requires intention and practice. Simple strategies, such as setting aside time for meditation, engaging in mindful movement, or practicing gratitude, can yield significant benefits over time. As we delve deeper into the specific techniques and practices that enhance mindfulness, readers will learn how to tailor these methods to their unique lifestyles and goals. By embracing mindfulness as a foundational aspect of personal and professional development, young professionals, entrepreneurs, and all individuals can unlock their full potential and navigate the challenges of life with greater ease and focus.

Meditation Practices for Improved Focus

Meditation has emerged as a powerful tool for enhancing focus and cognitive performance, particularly among young professionals, entrepreneurs, and students. In an increasingly fast-paced world, the ability to concentrate effectively is essential for success. Various meditation practices can help cultivate this skill by training the mind to remain present and engaged. By incorporating these techniques into daily routines, individuals can improve their mental acuity, reduce stress, and enhance decision-making capabilities.

One of the most accessible forms of meditation for improving focus is mindfulness meditation. This practice involves paying attention to the present moment without judgment, often focusing on the breath or bodily sensations. Regular mindfulness meditation can lead to significant improvements in attention span and cognitive flexibility, which are crucial for navigating the complexities of professional and academic environments. By dedicating just a few minutes each day to this practice, individuals can learn to redirect their thoughts and resist distractions, ultimately fostering a more productive mindset.

Another effective technique is focused attention meditation, where practitioners concentrate on a single object, sound, or thought for an extended period. This practice trains the mind to maintain focus and resist the urge to wander, enhancing mental discipline. For young professionals and entrepreneurs, honing this skill can be especially beneficial during critical tasks that require deep concentration, such as strategic planning or complex problem-solving. Over time, consistent practice can lead to lasting changes in brain function, making it easier to remain engaged in challenging tasks.

For those seeking a more dynamic approach, movement-based meditations like yoga or tai chi can also enhance focus. These practices combine physical activity with mindfulness, encouraging participants to synchronize their movements with their breath. This holistic approach not only boosts physical health but also sharpens mental clarity, making it an excellent choice for athletes and busy professionals alike. The integration of movement into meditation helps to release pent-up energy, allowing for a greater sense of calm and concentration afterward.

Lastly, guided meditations can be an excellent resource for individuals new to meditation or those looking to deepen their practice. These sessions, often led by experienced instructors, provide structured guidance on various focus-enhancing techniques. By listening to a guided meditation, practitioners can learn how to cultivate concentration in a supportive environment, making it a valuable tool for students preparing for exams or executives managing high-stakes projects. As individuals explore different meditation practices, they can discover what resonates most with them, ultimately tailoring their approach to suit their unique needs and goals in life.

Daily Mindfulness Routines

Daily Mindfulness Routines represent an essential component of personal and professional development, particularly for young professionals, entrepreneurs, and students seeking to enhance their cognitive capabilities. These routines foster a focused mindset, decrease stress levels, and improve overall mental clarity. The practice of mindfulness involves intentionally bringing one's attention to the present moment, allowing individuals to develop greater awareness of their thoughts, feelings, and surroundings. By incorporating mindfulness into daily routines, individuals can train their brains to operate more efficiently, thereby optimizing their decision-making processes and enhancing their performance in various aspects of life.

To effectively integrate mindfulness into a daily routine, one can start with simple practices that require minimal time yet yield significant benefits. For instance, beginning the day with a brief session of mindful breathing can set a positive tone for the hours ahead. This practice involves focusing on the breath, paying attention to the sensations of inhaling and exhaling, and gently bringing the mind back when distractions arise. This not only calms the mind but also cultivates a state of awareness that can be carried throughout the day. Research shows that even a few minutes of focused breathing can enhance neuroplasticity, enabling the brain to form new neural connections that improve focus and cognitive flexibility.

In addition to mindful breathing, incorporating mindfulness into routine activities can amplify its benefits. For example, engaging in mindful walking during breaks can be a powerful way to clear the mind and refresh one's focus. This practice involves paying attention to the physical sensations of walking-the movement of the legs, the contact of the feet with the ground, and the surrounding environment. Such activities not only serve as a mental reset but also promote physical health, linking the benefits of exercise with cognitive enhancement. Furthermore, this approach aligns with the understanding that physical activity positively influences brain function, making it a dual-purpose strategy for productivity and well- being.

Mindfulness can also be integrated into work and study sessions through techniques such as the Pomodoro Technique, which combines focused work intervals with short mindfulness breaks. After each 25-minute work session, taking a five-minute break to engage in a mindfulness exercise can help maintain high levels of focus and prevent burnout. This method not only encourages sustained concentration but also reinforces the habit of stepping back to assess one's mental state. By regularly checking in with oneself, individuals can recognize when they are becoming overwhelmed and need to recalibrate, thus improving time management and overall productivity.

Finally, the development of a consistent mindfulness routine can enhance emotional intelligence, an essential trait for young professionals and leaders. By fostering self- awareness and emotional regulation, mindfulness practices enable individuals to navigate interpersonal relationships more effectively, whether in a team setting or during negotiations. As emotional intelligence is a key driver of successful leadership and collaboration, cultivating this skill through daily mindfulness can lead to improved outcomes in both personal and professional interactions. By committing to mindfulness routines, individuals not only enhance their cognitive abilities but also position themselves for greater success in their careers and personal lives.

Chapter 4

Cognitive Behavioral Approaches to Goal Setting

Understanding Cognitive Behavioral Therapy (CBT)

Cognitive Behavioral Therapy (CBT) is a psychological approach that has gained significant recognition for its effectiveness in fostering mental resilience and enhancing cognitive function. At its core, CBT focuses on the interconnections between thoughts, feelings, and behaviors, offering a structured framework for individuals seeking to understand and modify their thought patterns. This is particularly relevant for young professionals, entrepreneurs, and students who often find themselves navigating high-stress environments and complex decision-making scenarios. By recognizing and challenging negative or distorted thought processes, individuals can foster a more positive mindset, ultimately leading to improved focus and productivity.

The principles of CBT are grounded in the concept of neuroplasticity, which refers to the brain's remarkable ability to reorganize itself in response to new experiences. This means that by engaging in CBT practices, individuals can not only change their immediate thought patterns but also create lasting changes in the brain that enhance cognitive performance. For young professionals and entrepreneurs, this translate into better problem-solving skills, heightened creativity, and improved emotional regulation-key components necessary for success in fast-paced environments. Understanding how to harness neuroplasticity through CBT techniques can empower individuals to make meaningful changes in their personal and professional lives.

Mindfulness and meditation are often integrated into CBT approaches, providing individuals with tools to enhance focus, reduce anxiety, and improve overall cognitive function. These practices encourage individuals to remain present and aware of their thoughts, allowing for greater self-reflection and the opportunity to challenge unhelpful beliefs. For students preparing for exams or professionals managing tight deadlines, incorporating mindfulness techniques can lead to improved concentration and a reduction in stress levels. By prioritizing mental clarity through mindfulness, individuals can approach challenges with a calm and focused mindset.

Goal setting is another critical area where CBT principles can be effectively applied. By utilizing cognitive behavioral approaches to establish clear, actionable goals, individuals can enhance their motivation and accountability. This method involves breaking down larger goals into smaller, manageable tasks while also addressing any cognitive distortions that may hinder progress. For executives and managers, applying these strategies can lead to more effective team leadership and improved project outcomes.

Understanding how to set realistic goals while maintaining a positive outlook is essential for sustaining motivation over time.

Finally, the integration of CBT with healthy lifestyle choices, such as proper nutrition and regular physical exercise, significantly contributes to cognitive enhancement. The brain thrives on a balanced diet rich in nutrients that support cognitive function and emotional health. Additionally, engaging in physical activity has been shown to improve mood and cognitive performance, creating a synergistic effect when combined with CBT practices. By adopting a holistic approach that includes cognitive behavioral techniques, mindfulness strategies, and healthy lifestyle choices, individuals can optimize their mental capabilities and achieve their personal and professional goals more effectively. This comprehensive understanding of CBT serves as a powerful tool for anyone looking to enhance their cognitive abilities and foster lasting success.

Setting SMART Goals

Setting SMART goals is a vital strategy for anyone looking to enhance their focus and achieve success, whether in their careers, studies, or personal development. The acronym SMART stands for Specific, Measurable, Achievable, Relevant, and Time-bound. This framework helps individuals clarify their objectives and create actionable plans that lead to tangible results. By understanding and applying each component of SMART goals, young professionals, entrepreneurs, students, and anyone interested in self-improvement can significantly enhance their mental acuity and decision-making skills.

Specificity is the first pillar of SMART goals and emphasizes the importance of having clear, well- defined objectives. Vague goals can lead to confusion and lack of direction, ultimately hindering progress. For instance, instead of stating, "I want to improve my focus," a more specific goal would be, "I will meditate for 10 minutes every morning to enhance my concentration." This level of specificity not only clarifies what needs to be achieved but also provides a clear target to aim for, making it easier to maintain focus and motivation.

The second element, Measurable, allows individuals to track their progress and determine whether they are on the right path. Measurable goals include quantifiable outcomes that can be monitored over time. For example, a student might set a goal to "read two academic papers per week" rather than simply stating an intention to read more. This measurable approach enables individuals to assess their performance, make necessary adjustments, and celebrate their successes, which can be crucial for maintaining motivation and commitment.

Achievable goals ensure that objectives are realistic and attainable, considering the resources and constraints that individuals may face. Setting overly ambitious goals can lead to frustration and burnout, while achievable goals foster a sense of accomplishment and growth. For example, an athlete might aim to improve their running time by a modest margin rather than attempting to achieve a world record overnight. This focus on achievability encourages steady progress and reinforces the belief that success is within reach, which is essential for building self-efficacy.

Relevance and Time-bound elements further enhance the effectiveness of SMART goals. Relevance ensures that the goals align with broader life ambitions and personal values, making the pursuit of these objectives more meaningful. Time- bound goals, on the other hand, create a sense of urgency and help individuals prioritize their efforts. For instance, setting a deadline such as "I will complete my business plan by the end of the month" instills a sense of accountability and encourages consistent action. By integrating these elements, individuals can create a structured approach to goal-setting that not only optimizes their cognitive function but also drives them toward sustained success in various aspects of their lives.

Actionable Plans for Personal and Professional Success

In the fast-paced world of personal professional development, creating actionable plans is essential for young professionals, entrepreneurs, students, and anyone seeking to optimize their cognitive abilities. Actionable plans are structured, clear steps that guide individuals toward achieving specific goals. By incorporating mindfulness techniques and cognitive behavioral approaches, these plans not only facilitate progress but also enhance mental acuity, focus, and decision-making skills. Understanding how to craft and implement these plans is crucial for fostering success and resilience in an ever-evolving landscape.

The foundation of an effective actionable plan lies in the principles of neuroplasticity. Recognizing that the brain can reorganize itself based on experiences and learning allows individuals to harness their potential for personal growth. By setting specific, measurable, achievable, relevant, and time-bound (SMART) goals, individuals can create a roadmap that aligns with their aspirations. For instance, a young professional might aim to enhance their public speaking skills. This goal can be broken down into smaller, actionable steps, such as enrolling in a public speaking course, practicing in front of peers, and seeking constructive feedback. Each step reinforces neural pathways associated with confidence and communication, leading to lasting improvements.

Mindfulness and meditation practices play a pivotal role in enhancing focus and reducing stress, making them integral to actionable plans. By integrating mindfulness techniques, individuals can cultivate greater awareness of their thoughts and emotions, which in turn supports better decision- making. For example, daily mindfulness meditation can help entrepreneurs develop clarity and focus, enabling them to prioritize tasks effectively. Implementing short mindfulness breaks throughout the day can also serve to reset the mind, allowing for a more productive work environment. These practices foster a resilient mindset, essential for navigating challenges and achieving long-term success.

Nutrition and physical exercise are critical components of cognitive performance that should not be overlooked in actionable plans. A balanced diet rich in nutrients supports brain health and enhances mental clarity. Incorporating foods high in omega-3 fatty acids, antioxidants, and vitamins can improve cognitive function and memory retention. Similarly, physical exercise has been shown to boost brain function by increasing blood flow and promoting the release of neurotrophic factors that support neural growth. Young professionals and entrepreneurs should consider integrating regular exercise routines and mindful eating habits into their plans, as these lifestyle choices can significantly enhance overall cognitive performance.

Lastly, effective time management strategies are essential for reducing overwhelm and increasing productivity. By evaluating how time is spent and identifying areas for improvement, individuals can create structured schedules that prioritize high- impact activities. Techniques such as the Pomodoro Technique, where work is divided into intervals with breaks, can enhance focus and prevent burnout. Additionally, establishing routines that incorporate sleep hygiene ensures that individuals are well-rested and mentally sharp. By aligning their time management strategies with their actionable plans, professionals can cultivate a sustainable path toward personal and professional success, ultimately leading to a more fulfilling and productive life.

Chapter 5

The Role of Nutrition in Cognitive Performance

The Connection Between Diet and Brain Health

The connection between diet and brain health is a pivotal aspect of cognitive performance that young professionals, entrepreneurs, and students alike should prioritize. Nutrition plays a crucial role in not only maintaining overall health but also in enhancing brain function. The brain, being an energy-intensive organ, requires a constant supply of nutrients to perform optimally. A balanced diet rich in essential fatty acids, vitamins, minerals, and antioxidants can significantly improve cognitive abilities, including memory, focus, and decision- making skills. Understanding how specific dietary components impact brain health can empower individuals to make informed choices that enhance their mental acuity.

One of the most significant dietary components influencing brain health is omega-3 fatty acids, primarily found in fatty fish such as salmon, walnuts, and flaxseeds. These healthy fats are critical for maintaining the structural integrity of brain cells and facilitating communication between them. Research indicates that omega-3s can enhance neuroplasticity-the brain's ability to reorganize itself by forming new neural connections -which is essential for learning and memory. This is particularly relevant for students and entrepreneurs who are constantly acquiring new skills and knowledge. Incorporating omega-3-rich foods into one's diet can lead to improvements in cognitive function and emotional well-being.

In addition to omega-3 fatty acids, antioxidants found in fruits and vegetables play a vital role in protecting the brain from oxidative stress. Foods rich in antioxidants, such as berries, dark chocolate, and leafy greens, help combat inflammation and reduce the risk of neurodegenerative diseases. This is particularly important for professionals in high- stress environments, where cognitive overload can lead to diminished performance. By consuming a diet high in antioxidants, individuals can better manage stress and maintain sharper focus throughout their workday, ultimately enhancing productivity and decision-making capabilities.

Furthermore, the role of hydration in brain health cannot be overlooked. The brain is composed of approximately 75% water, and even mild dehydration can impair cognitive functions such as concentration, memory, and mood. Young professionals and entrepreneurs, often juggling multiple tasks and deadlines, must prioritize hydration to maintain optimal brain function. Drinking sufficient water throughout the day, alongside a diet inclusive of hydrating foods like fruits and vegetables, supports cognitive clarity and helps prevent fatigue.

Lastly, the impact of diet on mental health and emotional well-being is an essential consideration for anyone looking to enhance their overall cognitive performance. Nutritional deficiencies can lead to mood disorders, anxiety, and other mental health issues that can significantly hinder professional and personal growth. By focusing on a well-rounded diet that includes whole grains, lean proteins, healthy fats, and plenty of fruits and vegetables, individuals can not only improve their brain health but also foster resilience and stability in their emotional lives. Embracing dietary changes as part of a holistic approach to personal development can create a solid foundation for success in various aspects of life, from academia to entrepreneurship and beyond.

Nutrients that Enhance Cognitive Function

In the pursuit of cognitive enhancement, understanding the role of nutrition is paramount. The brain, being an energy-intensive organ, relies heavily on various nutrients to function optimally. Essential nutrients such as omega-3 fatty acids, antioxidants, vitamins, and minerals play a vital role in promoting cognitive health. Omega-3s, found in fatty fish like salmon and walnuts, are particularly significant for brain structure and function, contributing to improved memory and learning capabilities. These fatty acids support the maintenance of neuronal membranes, ensuring effective communication between brain cells, which is crucial for cognitive processes.

Antioxidants, including vitamins C and E, are also critical in combating oxidative stress, a condition linked to cognitive decline. Foods rich in antioxidants, such as berries, dark chocolate, and green leafy vegetables, help protect brain cells from damage caused by free radicals. By incorporating these foods into their diets, young professionals, entrepreneurs, and students can enhance their brain's resilience and promote long-term cognitive health. Moreover, a diet high in fruits and vegetables not only provides essential vitamins but also supports overall well-being, which is inherently tied to mental clarity and focus.

B vitamins, particularly B6, B12, and folate, are fundamental for brain health and cognitive function. These vitamins contribute to the production of neurotransmitters, which are chemicals responsible for transmitting signals in the brain. A deficiency in these nutrients can lead to decreased cognitive performance and increased levels of fatigue. Young professionals and executives should prioritize foods such as eggs, legumes, and whole grains, which are abundant in B vitamins, to sustain their mental acuity and productivity. Furthermore, the inclusion of these nutrients in the diet can support emotional well-being, an essential aspect for maintaining high performance in demanding environments.

Minerals like iron and magnesium also play a significant role in cognitive processes. Iron is crucial for oxygen transport in the blood, which is vital for brain function, while magnesium helps regulate neurotransmitters that send signals throughout the nervous system. A diet lacking in these minerals can lead to cognitive impairments, reduced focus, and increased anxiety, making it essential for individuals in high-pressure situations, such as entrepreneurs and executives, to ensure they are consuming adequate amounts of these nutrients. Foods rich in iron, such as lean meats and spinach, alongside magnesium sources like nuts and seeds, should be staples in their diets.

Ultimately, the integration of a nutrient-rich diet can significantly enhance cognitive function, supporting the goals of young professionals, entrepreneurs, students, and others striving for personal and professional success. By understanding the specific nutrients that contribute to brain health and making conscious dietary choices, individuals can optimize their mental capabilities. This, in turn, fosters not only improved focus and decision-making but also a more resilient mindset, essential for navigating the challenges of both academic and professional life. Investing in nutritional knowledge and habits is a powerful step towards maximizing cognitive potential and achieving desired outcomes in one's career and personal life.

Meal Planning for Optimal Mental Clarity

Meal planning plays a pivotal role in enhancing mental clarity and cognitive function, particularly for young professionals and entrepreneurs who are constantly under pressure to perform at their best. The brain requires specific nutrients to function optimally, and the foods we consume directly impact our mood, focus, and overall cognitive capabilities. By strategically planning meals, individuals can ensure they are fueling their brains with the right nutrients to support mental acuity, boost productivity, and enhance decision-making skills.

A well-balanced diet rich in whole foods, such as fruits, vegetables, whole grains, lean proteins, and healthy fats, is essential for maintaining cognitive health. These foods provide vital vitamins and minerals necessary for brain function. For instance, omega-3 fatty acids found in fatty fish, flaxseeds, and walnuts are known to support cognitive performance and reduce the risk of cognitive decline. Additionally, antioxidants present in colorful fruits and vegetables help combat oxidative stress, which can impair brain function. By incorporating these nutrient-dense foods into meal plans, individuals can create a solid foundation for optimal mental clarity.

In addition to the types of foods consumed, the timing of meals also plays an important role in cognitive performance. Regular meal intervals help maintain stable blood sugar levels, which are crucial for sustaining energy and focus throughout the day. Skipping meals or consuming high-sugar snacks can lead to energy spikes and crashes, negatively affecting concentration and productivity. Planning meals and snacks at regular intervals can help manage energy levels and ensure that the brain receives a steady supply of nutrients, promoting sustained mental clarity.

Hydration is another key component of meal planning that often gets overlooked. The brain is composed of approximately 75% water, and even mild dehydration can lead to cognitive impairments, including difficulty concentrating and reduced memory retention. Including hydration as part of a meal planning routine, whether through water-rich foods or adequate fluid intake, is essential for maintaining optimal brain function. Young professionals and students should prioritize hydration before, during, and after meals to keep their cognitive abilities sharp.

Finally, meal planning can be an opportunity for mindfulness and intentional living. By taking the time to prepare meals, individuals can cultivate a greater awareness of their food choices and the impact those choices have on their mental well- being. Incorporating mindfulness practices into the meal preparation process can help reduce stress and enhance focus, further contributing to overall cognitive performance. By viewing meal planning not just as a necessity but as a powerful tool for nurturing brain health, young professionals and entrepreneurs can set themselves up for success in both personal and professional endeavors.

Chapter 6

Physical Exercise and Brain Function

How Exercise Affects Cognitive Enhancement

Exercise has long been recognized for its physical benefits, but its impact on cognitive function is equally profound and multifaceted. Engaging in regular physical activity can lead to significant enhancements in mental acuity, memory, and overall brain health. For young professionals, entrepreneurs, students, and anyone seeking to optimize their cognitive abilities, understanding how exercise influences brain function is crucial. This knowledge can empower individuals to incorporate exercise into their daily routines, thereby reaping the rewards of improved focus and decision-making skills.

Research has demonstrated that physical exercise prompts a cascade of biochemical processes that promote brain health. When we engage in activities like running, swimming, or even brisk walking, our bodies release endorphins and other neurochemicals such as brain-derived neurotrophic factor (BDNF). BDNF plays a critical role in neuroplasticity, the brain's ability to reorganize itself by forming new neural connections. This process not only supports learning and memory but also enhances resilience against cognitive decline. For young professionals and students, integrating exercise into their schedules can serve as a powerful tool for enhancing cognitive performance and boosting productivity.

Furthermore, regular physical activity has been shown to improve mood and reduce symptoms of anxiety and depression. The mental clarity that follows a workout can lead to better focus and creativity, essential traits for entrepreneurs and executives alike. Increased blood flow to the brain during exercise also promotes the delivery of oxygen and nutrients, which are vital for optimal cognitive function. As such, incorporating short bursts of exercise throughout the day can lead to a noticeable improvement in mental clarity, making it easier to tackle complex tasks or engage in strategic thinking.

In addition to the immediate cognitive benefits, exercise can also foster long-term brain health. Studies indicate that a consistent exercise regimen can help ward off age-related cognitive decline and neurodegenerative diseases. This insight is particularly relevant for those in leadership positions, where strategic thinking and decision- making are paramount. By prioritizing physical fitness, executives and managers can not only enhance their own cognitive capabilities but also model healthy behaviors for their teams, creating a culture of wellness and productivity.

To fully harness the cognitive-enhancing effects of exercise, individuals should aim for a balanced approach that includes both aerobic and strength- training activities. Mindfulness practices, when combined with physical exercise, can further amplify cognitive benefits. For personal development enthusiasts and anyone eager to improve their mental faculties, the integration of exercise, mindfulness, and proper nutrition provides a holistic strategy for achieving personal and professional goals. Ultimately, recognizing the profound connection between physical activity and cognitive enhancement can transform one's approach to personal growth and success in all areas of life.

Types of Physical Activities for Brain Health

Physical activity is often associated with physical fitness, but its benefits extend far beyond the body. Engaging in different types of physical activities can significantly enhance brain health, making it a vital component of a holistic approach to personal and professional development. For young professionals, entrepreneurs, students, and anyone seeking to boost cognitive function, understanding the various types of physical activities available can help in choosing the right ones to support mental acuity and overall well-being.

Aerobic exercise is one of the most effective forms of physical activity for brain health. Activities such as running, cycling, swimming, and even brisk walking increase the heart rate and improve circulation, facilitating the flow of oxygen and nutrients to the brain. Studies have shown that regular aerobic exercise can enhance neurogenesis -the process of creating new neurons—as well as increase the production of brain-derived neurotrophic factor (BDNF), a protein that supports the survival of existing neurons and encourages the growth of new ones. These benefits can lead to improved memory, better learning capabilities, and enhanced problem-solving skills, all of which are crucial for young professionals and entrepreneurs striving for excellence in their fields.

Strength training, often overlooked in discussions about brain health, also plays a significant role. Engaging in resistance exercises, such as weightlifting or bodyweight workouts, can boost cognition by improving motor control and coordination. Moreover, strength training has been linked to increased levels of hormones such as testosterone and growth hormone, both of which can enhance brain function. For executives and managers, incorporating strength training into their routine can lead to sharper decision-making skills and increased resilience under pressure, supporting their leadership roles.

Mindful movement practices, including yoga and tai chi, offer unique cognitive benefits as well. These activities emphasize the connection between mind and body, promoting awareness and enhancing focus through deliberate movements and breathing techniques. The meditative aspects of these practices can reduce stress and anxiety, which are often barriers to optimal cognitive performance. Students preparing for exams or professionals facing high-pressure situations can find that incorporating mindful movement into their routines not only improves mental clarity but also cultivates emotional resilience.

Lastly, recreational activities that involve social interaction, such as team sports or group fitness classes, can also contribute to brain health. Engaging in physical activities with others fosters a sense of community and belonging, which are essential for emotional well-being. The social aspect of these activities can enhance motivation and accountability, making it easier for individuals to maintain their exercise routines. As personal development enthusiasts and athletes alike understand, the benefits of physical activity extend beyond the individual; they ripple through our social networks, enhancing overall cognitive function and emotional intelligence in both personal and professional contexts. By integrating a variety of physical activities into daily routines, individuals can harness the full potential of their brain while laying the groundwork for success.

Creating an Exercise Routine for Mental Well-Being

Creating an exercise routine for mental well-being is a vital component in the journey toward enhanced cognitive function and overall mental health. Physical activity has been extensively studied and recognized for its profound effects on the brain, particularly in young professionals, entrepreneurs, students, and anyone seeking personal development. Engaging in regular exercise not only improves physical fitness but also fosters neuroplasticity-the brain's ability to reorganize itself-enhancing mental acuity and resilience. By establishing an exercise routine that prioritizes both physical and mental well-being, individuals can lay the groundwork for achieving their personal and professional goals.

To create an effective exercise routine, one must first consider personal preferences and accessibility. Whether it's running, yoga, weight training, or team sports, choosing activities that resonate with individual interests can significantly increase adherence to the routine. For young professionals and entrepreneurs who often juggle busy schedules, integrating short bursts of physical activity into daily routines can be particularly beneficial. Even 10 to 15 minutes of focused exercise can elevate mood, boost energy, and sharpen focus, making it easier to tackle demanding tasks and improve decision-making skills.

Mindfulness and meditation practices can be seamlessly integrated into physical exercise routines to amplify their benefits. Techniques such as yoga or tai chi not only promote physical strength but also enhance mental clarity and emotional regulation. These practices encourage individuals to cultivate a present-moment awareness that serves as a powerful antidote to stress and anxiety. As a result, participants may find they are better equipped to handle the pressures of academic life, business challenges, or leadership responsibilities. Incorporating mindfulness into exercise routines fosters a holistic approach to well-being, aligning physical health with mental clarity.

Nutrition also plays a crucial role in optimizing the benefits of an exercise routine for mental well- being. A balanced diet rich in omega-3 fatty acids, antioxidants, and essential vitamins can significantly enhance cognitive function and resilience. Young professionals and students should pay attention to their nutritional intake, ensuring that they fuel their bodies with the right nutrients to support their mental and physical activities. The synergy between exercise and proper nutrition creates a comprehensive strategy for cognitive enhancement, resulting in improved focus, memory, and overall mental performance.

In conclusion, creating an exercise routine for mental well-being is not merely about physical conditioning but rather a holistic approach to enhancing cognitive capabilities. By choosing enjoyable activities, incorporating mindfulness practices, and maintaining a balanced diet, individuals can optimize their mental acuity and resilience. This multifaceted routine can help young professionals, students, entrepreneurs, and anyone dedicated to personal development achieve their goals while maintaining a sharp, focused mind. As the understanding of the connection between physical exercise and mental health deepens, it becomes increasingly clear that an intentional exercise routine is a powerful tool for fostering success in all areas of life.

Chapter 7

Memory Enhancement Techniques

Understanding Memory and Its Importance

Memory is a fundamental cognitive function that plays a crucial role in our daily lives, influencing how we learn, make decisions, and interact with the world. Understanding memory involves recognizing its various types, such as short-term and long-term memory, and the processes involved in encoding, storing, and retrieving information. For young professionals, entrepreneurs, students, and anyone keen on self-improvement, this understanding is vital. A robust memory enhances one's ability to acquire new skills, recall essential information during critical moments, and ultimately achieve personal and professional goals.

The importance of memory extends beyond mere information retention; it is deeply intertwined with our identity and how we navigate our experiences. Memory shapes our perceptions and informs our decision-making processes. For instance, when entrepreneurs strategize for their businesses, they draw on past experiences, market trends, and learned knowledge to make informed choices. Similarly, students rely on their memory to absorb complex concepts and prepare for exams effectively. Thus, enhancing memory can significantly impact success across various fields, underpinning the importance of memory optimization techniques.

Neuroplasticity, the brain's remarkable ability to reorganize itself by forming new neural connections, offers exciting possibilities for memory enhancement. Young professionals and entrepreneurs can leverage this concept to train their brains intentionally. By engaging in activities that challenge cognitive abilities, such as learning new skills or languages, individuals can foster brain adaptability. This principle also extends mindfulness practices that promote focus and awareness, thereby improving memory retention. Embracing neuroplasticity techniques can lead to improved performance and resilience, enabling individuals to adapt to the fast-paced demands of their careers.

Mindfulness and meditation practices are particularly effective in sharpening memory and cognitive function. These techniques encourage individuals to cultivate present-moment awareness, reducing distractions that can impair memory recall. Regular mindfulness practice has been shown to enhance attention span and cognitive flexibility, making it easier to absorb and retain information. For executives and managers, incorporating mindfulness into their routine can improve decision-making skills and foster a more productive work environment. The ability to remain focused amidst the chaos can transform how leaders operate, allowing them to make strategic choices based on clear and accurate information.

Finally, memory enhancement is not solely about mental exercises; it is also influenced by physical health and lifestyle choices. Nutrition plays a pivotal role in cognitive performance, with specific diets linked to improved brain function. Additionally, regular physical exercise has been shown to boost memory by increasing blood flow to the brain and promoting the growth of new neurons. For athletes, integrating mental conditioning with physical training can lead to peak performance, while for young professionals and students, adopting a holistic approach to brain health can facilitate sustained cognitive enhancement. By understanding and optimizing memory, individuals can unlock their potential and pave the way for lasting success.

Techniques for Improving Memory Retention

Memory retention is a crucial skill for young professionals, entrepreneurs, students, and anyone striving for personal or professional development. Improving memory not only enhances learning and recall but also plays a significant role in decision- making and problem-solving. As we delve into techniques for improving memory retention, it's important to understand that these methods can be adapted to fit various lifestyles and preferences, making them accessible to a wide audience.

One effective technique for enhancing memory retention is the use of mnemonic devices. Mnemonics are memory aids that facilitate the recall of information through association. For example, acronyms, rhymes, or visual imagery can help individuals remember complex information more easily. Young professionals and students can benefit greatly from these tools when studying or preparing for presentations. By transforming abstract concepts into relatable and memorable formats, mnemonics can significantly boost cognitive performance and retention.

Incorporating mindfulness and meditation practices is another powerful strategy for improving memory. These techniques not only promote relaxation but also enhance focus and cognitive function. Mindfulness encourages individuals to be present in the moment, which can reduce distractions and improve the ability to absorb and retain information. Regular meditation practice has been shown to enhance neuroplasticity, the brain's ability to reorganize itself, making it more adept at forming and recalling memories. This is particularly beneficial for entrepreneurs and executives who require sharp mental acuity for strategic decision- making.

Physical exercise also plays a vital role in memory enhancement. Engaging in regular physical activity increases blood flow to the brain, which can improve cognitive function and memory retention. Activities like aerobic exercises, yoga, or even short walks can stimulate the release of neurotrophic factors that promote brain health. For athletes and professionals in high-pressure environments, maintaining a consistent exercise routine can complement mental training, ensuring that both body and mind are in peak condition for performance.

Finally, the role of nutrition in cognitive performance cannot be overlooked. A balanced diet rich in omega-3 fatty acids, antioxidants, and vitamins is essential for optimal brain health. Foods such as fatty fish, nuts, berries, and leafy greens contribute to improved memory and cognitive function. Young professionals and students should be mindful of their dietary choices, as proper nutrition can enhance focus, reduce fatigue, and improve overall mental clarity. By combining these various techniques-mnemonics, mindfulness, physical exercise, and good nutrition-individuals can create a comprehensive approach to improving memory retention that supports their personal and professional goals.

Tools and Resources for Better Recall

In the journey towards better recall and cognitive performance, young professionals, entrepreneurs, students, and anyone keen on personal development can leverage various tools and resources designed to enhance memory retention and retrieval. Understanding and implementing these strategies can significantly boost productivity and decision-making abilities, ultimately leading to greater success in both personal and professional realms. This subchapter will explore effective memory enhancement techniques, drawing from neuroscience, mindfulness practices, and cognitive behavioral approaches.

One of the most powerful tools in memory enhancement is the technique of spaced repetition. This method capitalizes on the brain's natural ability to retain information over time by revisiting material at gradually increasing intervals. For students preparing for exams or professionals absorbing new information, apps like Anki or Quizlet can facilitate this process. By structuring study or training sessions to include spaced repetition, individuals can transform how they absorb and recall information, leading to improved academic performance and sharper business acumen.

Mindfulness and meditation practices also play a crucial role in enhancing cognitive function and memory recall. Engaging in regular mindfulness exercises helps develop a heightened awareness of thoughts and feelings, which can translate into better focus and retention of information. Techniques such as focused breathing or body scans can reduce stress, a known impediment to effective memory functioning. Resources like guided meditation apps, such as Headspace or Calm, provide structured approaches to incorporating mindfulness into daily routines, making it easier for professionals and students alike to integrate these practices into their lives.

Nutrition is another essential element in the quest for enhanced cognitive abilities. The brain requires specific nutrients to function optimally, and certain foods can directly influence memory and focus. Omega-3 fatty acids, found in fish and nuts, are linked to improved cognitive performance, while antioxidants from fruits and vegetables can protect brain cells from damage. Young professionals and entrepreneurs should consider not only what they eat but also how their dietary choices can impact their mental acuity. Consulting resources on nutritional neuroscience can provide valuable insights into optimizing diet for better brain health.

Physical exercise, often overlooked in cognitive discussions, is vital for brain function. Regular aerobic activity has been shown to enhance memory and cognitive performance by promoting the flow of oxygen-rich blood to the brain. Incorporating movement into daily routines - whether through structured workouts or simple activities like walking - can lead to significant improvements in focus and memory recall. Tools such as fitness trackers can help individuals monitor their activity levels, ensuring they maintain a consistent exercise regimen tailored to boost cognitive abilities.

In addition to these strategies, developing emotional intelligence through self-awareness and regulation can further enhance memory and decision-making skills. Understanding one's emotional responses can lead to better focus and recall, particularly in high-pressure situations. Creating a reflective practice, such as journaling or engaging in feedback sessions, allows individuals to cultivate emotional awareness, which can be a powerful ally in both personal and professional development. By harnessing these tools and resources, young professionals, entrepreneurs, and students can foster a mindset that not only values memory enhancement but also drives them toward success in their respective fields.

Chapter 8

Emotional Intelligence Development

Defining Intelligence Emotional

Emotional intelligence (EI) is a vital skill set that encompasses the ability to recognize, understand, and manage our own emotions while also being attuned to the emotions of others. In today's fast- paced environment, particularly for young professionals, entrepreneurs, and students, the importance of EI cannot be overstated. It serves as a framework for navigating complex social interactions, fostering collaboration, and enhancing decision-making capabilities. EI is not merely about being "nice" or empathetic; it is a structured approach to understanding emotional cues that significantly impact personal and professional relationships.

At its core, emotional intelligence consists of four key components: self-awareness, self-regulation, social awareness, and relationship management. Self-awareness involves recognizing one's emotions and how they influence thoughts and behaviors. This foundational skill allows individuals to accurately assess their strengths and weaknesses, leading to a more authentic and confident self- presentation. Self-regulation follows, enabling the management of emotions in a constructive manner, which is particularly important in high-pressure situations often faced by young professionals and entrepreneurs. This control over one's emotional responses fosters resilience and adaptability, essential traits in any career.

Social awareness, the third component, extends the concept of EI beyond the self to the broader social context. It involves the ability to empathize with others and understand their emotional needs and perspectives. For students and entrepreneurs, honing social awareness can lead to better teamwork, effective networking, and stronger customer relations. This dimension of EI enhances one's capacity to read social cues and respond appropriately, which is increasingly crucial in diverse and collaborative environments. Those who cultivate social awareness are often more adept at building rapport and trust, essential elements for any successful relationship.

The final component, relationship management, ties together the skills of emotional intelligence to enable effective communication and conflict resolution. This aspect is particularly important for executives and managers who must lead teams, inspire others, and navigate the complexities of organizational dynamics. Mastering relationship management not only enhances leadership effectiveness but also contributes to a positive workplace culture. For athletes, this skill can translate into improved team dynamics and performance, showcasing the universal applicability of EI across various fields.

Building emotional intelligence is a deliberate practice that can significantly enhance cognitive performance and overall success. Techniques such as mindfulness meditation can help individuals develop self-awareness and emotional regulation, while cognitive behavioral strategies can aid in reframing negative thoughts and responses. By integrating these practices into daily routines, young professionals, students, and anyone committed to personal development can cultivate a robust emotional intelligence that not only enriches their own lives but also positively impacts those around them, creating a ripple effect of growth and collaboration in their personal and professional spheres.

Techniques for Building Emotional Awareness

Building emotional awareness is a crucial skill for young professionals, entrepreneurs, students, and anyone aiming to improve their mental acuity and interpersonal relationships. Emotional awareness involves recognizing and understanding one's own emotions, as well as the emotions of others, which can significantly influence decision-making, communication, and leadership. By cultivating this awareness, individuals can create a more empathetic and productive work environment, enhance their personal relationships, and foster resilience in the face of challenges.

One effective technique for building emotional awareness is the practice of mindfulness. Mindfulness encourages individuals to observe their thoughts and feelings without judgment, creating a space for reflection and understanding. This practice can be integrated into daily routines through simple exercises such as mindful breathing, where one focuses on their breath to center themselves. By regularly engaging in mindfulness, young professionals and entrepreneurs can develop a heightened sensitivity to their emotional states, allowing them to respond thoughtfully rather than react impulsively in various situations.

Another powerful approach to enhance emotional awareness is journaling. Writing about daily experiences and emotions can help individuals process their feelings and identify patterns in their emotional responses. This practice encourages introspection and can lead to greater self- understanding. For students and personal development enthusiasts, journaling serves as a tool to track progress over time, analyze emotional triggers, and set intentions for future growth. By articulating emotions on paper, individuals can clarify their thoughts and cultivate a deeper connection with their emotional landscape.

Engaging in active listening is also vital for developing emotional awareness, particularly in interpersonal relationships and professional settings. This technique involves fully concentrating on what others are saying, reflecting on their emotions, and responding empathetically. By practicing active listening, individuals can better understand the emotions and perspectives of colleagues, clients, or peers, which is essential for effective collaboration and leadership. This skill is especially beneficial for executives and managers, as it promotes a culture of openness and fosters stronger team dynamics.

Lastly, incorporating feedback into one's emotional development can significantly enhance awareness. Seeking constructive criticism from trusted peers or mentors allows individuals to gain insights into how their emotions and behaviors are perceived by others. This external perspective can illuminate blind spots and encourage growth in emotional intelligence. By embracing feedback as a valuable tool for self-improvement, professionals and entrepreneurs can refine their emotional responses, improve their leadership capabilities, and ultimately create more meaningful connections in both personal and professional spheres.

Enhancing Leadership Skills Through Emotional Regulation

Emotional regulation is a critical skill for effective leadership, particularly for young professionals and entrepreneurs navigating the complexities of their careers. It involves the ability to manage and respond to one's emotions in a constructive manner, allowing leaders to maintain composure under pressure, make informed decisions, and foster a positive work environment. By enhancing emotional regulation, individuals can not only improve their leadership capabilities but also cultivate stronger relationships with team members, clients, and stakeholders. This skill is particularly vital in high-stress situations where emotional responses can significantly impact decision-making and outcomes.

One of the most powerful aspects of emotional regulation is its connection to emotional intelligence, which encompasses the ability to recognize, understand, and influence emotions in oneself and others. Young professionals and entrepreneurs can benefit greatly from developing this capacity, as it enables them to navigate interpersonal dynamics with greater skill. Techniques such as mindfulness and reflection can aid in enhancing emotional awareness, helping individuals identify their emotional triggers and responses. By acknowledging these triggers, leaders can better anticipate their reactions and choose responses that align with their goals and values.

Incorporating mindfulness practices into daily routines can significantly enhance emotional regulation. Mindfulness encourages individuals to stay present and grounded, reducing impulsivity and fostering thoughtful decision-making. Daily meditation, for example, can help individuals cultivate a calm and focused mindset, making it easier to respond to challenging situations with clarity rather than reactivity. Furthermore, mindfulness practices can reduce stress and anxiety, which are often barriers to effective emotional regulation, allowing leaders to approach challenges with a more balanced perspective.

Another aspect of emotional regulation involves developing resilience, which is the ability to bounce back from setbacks and maintain motivation in the face of adversity. Young professionals and entrepreneurs often face numerous challenges, from project deadlines to financial pressures. By focusing on resilience-building techniques, such as reframing negative thoughts and practicing self-compassion, individuals can enhance their capacity to cope with stress and maintain emotional equilibrium. This resilience not only supports personal well-being but also sets a positive example for team members, fostering a culture of perseverance and adaptability.

Ultimately, enhancing leadership skills through emotional regulation is a multifaceted process that involves self-awareness, mindfulness, and resilience. By investing time and effort into developing these skills, young professionals, entrepreneurs, and leaders can create a solid foundation for successful careers. The ability to manage emotions effectively not only enhances personal performance but also contributes to a more harmonious and productive work environment. As individuals cultivate these skills, they become better equipped to inspire and guide others, paving the way for collective success and growth in their professional journeys.

Chapter 9

The Science of Habits and Routines

Understanding Habit Formation

Understanding habit formation is crucial for young professionals, entrepreneurs, students, and anyone keen on personal development. Habits are the building blocks of our daily routines, influencing our behaviors, decision-making processes, and ultimately, our success. At their core, habits are automatic responses that require minimal cognitive effort once established. This automaticity is what makes habits powerful; they allow us to navigate our lives efficiently, freeing up mental resources for more complex tasks. By understanding the underlying mechanisms of habit formation, individuals can strategically cultivate positive habits that align with their goals.

The process of habit formation can be broken down into three main components: cue, routine, and reward. The cue is a trigger that initiates the habit; it can be anything from a specific time of day, an emotional state, or a preceding action. The routine is the behavior itself-what we do in response to the cue. Finally, the reward is the positive reinforcement that follows the routine, reinforcing the behavior and making it more likely to occur again in the future. This cyclical nature of habits is deeply rooted in our brain's neuroplasticity, which refers to the brain's ability to reorganize and adapt its pathways based on experience. By leveraging this understanding, individuals can design their environments to cultivate cues that promote desirable routines and rewards that enhance motivation.

Mindfulness plays a significant role in habit formation by fostering awareness of our automatic behaviors. Through mindfulness practices, individuals can become more attuned to their triggers and routines, allowing them to make conscious choices rather than automatic responses. For instance, a young professional may find themselves reaching for unhealthy snacks during work hours out of habit. By practicing mindfulness, they can identify the cue-perhaps stress or boredom-and consciously choose a healthier alternative, thereby reshaping their routine. This awareness not only aids in habit modification but also enhances emotional regulation, which is vital for maintaining focus and productivity.

Furthermore, the integration of cognitive-behavioral approaches can significantly enhance habit formation. Cognitive Behavioral Therapy (CBT) emphasizes the connection between thoughts, feelings, and behaviors. By identifying negative thought patterns that undermine positive habits, individuals can develop actionable strategies to counteract these mindsets. For example, a student preparing for exams may struggle with procrastination due to fear of failure. By using CBT techniques, they can reframe their thoughts, focusing on progress rather than perfection, which in turn fosters a more productive study routine. This cognitive restructuring is essential for sustaining motivation and achieving long-term success.

Lastly, the role of nutrition and physical exercise in habit formation cannot be overlooked. A well-balanced diet provides the essential nutrients that support cognitive function, while regular physical activity enhances overall brain health. These lifestyle factors not only improve mental clarity and focus but can also serve as cues for establishing productive habits. For instance, incorporating a morning workout routine can act as a powerful cue, prompting individuals to engage in other positive behaviors throughout the day. By understanding the interplay between habits, mindfulness, cognitive strategies, and lifestyle choices, individuals can create a comprehensive framework for personal and professional growth that cultivates success in all facets of life.

Strategies for Establishing Productive Habits

Establishing productive habits is a cornerstone of success for young professionals, entrepreneurs, and anyone striving for personal development. A well-structured approach to habit formation can significantly enhance cognitive abilities and overall performance. The first step in this process is understanding the science behind habits and routines. Habits are automatic behaviors that arise from repeated actions, and they can either propel you toward your goals or hinder your progress. By leveraging the principles of neuroplasticity, individuals can rewire their brains to support positive habits, fostering resilience and adaptability in the face of challenges.

Creating a conducive environment is essential for habit formation. Surrounding yourself with cues that promote positive behavior can make the process smoother. For instance, if you're looking to improve your focus during work hours, consider organizing your workspace to minimize distractions. This may involve decluttering your desk, utilizing noise-canceling headphones, or designating specific times for checking emails and social media. By establishing a physical environment that aligns with your goals, you create a supportive backdrop that encourages productive habits and reduces the cognitive load associated with decision-making.

Mindfulness and meditation practices play a crucial role in establishing productive habits. These techniques help individuals enhance their focus and reduce stress, which can otherwise derail progress. By incorporating short mindfulness exercises into your daily routine, you can improve your mental clarity and emotional regulation. For instance, practicing deep breathing or engaging in a brief meditation session before tackling a challenging task can center your mind and prepare you for optimal performance. These moments of mindfulness not only enhance your ability to concentrate but also cultivate a greater awareness of your thoughts and behaviors, allowing for more intentional habit formation.

Goal setting is another vital strategy for establishing productive habits. Utilizing cognitive behavioral approaches can help you create actionable and realistic plans that align with your personal and professional aspirations. Break down larger goals into smaller, manageable tasks, and establish specific timelines for completion. This method not only makes the goals more attainable but also provides opportunities for regular reflection and adjustment. Celebrating small victories along the way can reinforce positive behaviors and motivate you to maintain your momentum, ultimately leading to the development of lasting habits.

Lastly, integrating physical exercise and nutrition into your daily routine is essential for cognitive enhancement and sustaining productivity. Regular physical activity has been shown to improve brain function, boost mood, and enhance overall well- being. Similarly, a balanced diet rich in nutrients can significantly impact cognitive performance. Prioritizing sleep hygiene also plays a critical role in maximizing cognitive abilities. By ensuring you are well-rested, you create the ideal conditions for your brain to thrive. Together, these strategies form a holistic approach to establishing productive habits that not only support success but also promote long-term personal growth and fulfillment.

Maintaining Motivation Through Routine

Maintaining motivation through routine is a cornerstone of personal and professional success, particularly for young professionals, entrepreneurs, and students who are navigating the challenges of their respective journeys. A well-structured routine serves as a framework that not only helps in managing time effectively but also fosters an environment conducive to focus and productivity. By establishing consistent daily habits, individuals can create a predictable pattern that minimizes decision fatigue, allowing their mental resources to be allocated towards more complex and creative tasks. This routine acts as a stabilizing force, enabling one to maintain motivation even during challenging periods.

The science of habits and routines reveals that the brain responds positively to repetition and structure. Neuroplasticity, the brain's ability to reorganize itself by forming new neural connections, plays a vital role in this process. When individuals engage in consistent routines, they are essentially training their brains to function more efficiently. Each time a task is repeated, the neural pathways associated with that activity become stronger, making the behavior more automatic over time. This not only enhances performance but also builds resilience, as individuals become more adept at handling stress and adapting to new challenges that may arise in their personal or professional lives.

Mindfulness techniques integrated into daily routines can further enhance motivation. Taking time to practice mindfulness and meditation can improve focus, reduce stress, and enhance cognitive function, leading to greater clarity in decision-making. These practices encourage individuals to be present in the moment, fostering a deeper awareness of their thoughts and feelings. By incorporating mindfulness into their routines, young professionals and entrepreneurs can cultivate a positive mindset that fuels their motivation, allowing them to remain committed to their goals even when faced with obstacles.

Furthermore, the role of nutrition and physical exercise in maintaining motivation cannot be overlooked. A balanced diet rich in nutrients supports cognitive performance, while regular physical activity has been shown to boost mood and improve mental clarity. By prioritizing nutrition and exercise within their routines, individuals can optimize their brain function and emotional well- being. This holistic approach ensures that both the mind and body are prepared to tackle the demands of their professional or academic lives, ultimately leading to sustained motivation and success.

Finally, effective time management strategies are essential for optimizing routines. Learning to prioritize tasks, set achievable goals, and allocate time wisely can significantly reduce feelings of overwhelm. By incorporating time management techniques into their daily schedules, young professionals and entrepreneurs can create a sense of control over their responsibilities, which in turn fosters motivation. The combination of structured routines, mindfulness practices, healthy habits, and effective time management creates a powerful synergy that not only enhances cognitive abilities but also propels individuals toward their personal and professional aspirations.

Chapter 10

Time Management for Brain Optimization

The Importance of Effective Time Management

Effective time management is a cornerstone of success for young professionals, entrepreneurs, and anyone striving to achieve personal or professional goals. In a fast-paced world filled with distractions, mastering the ability to manage one's time can lead to increased productivity, reduced stress, and improved overall performance. Time management enables individuals to allocate their resources wisely, ensuring that they focus on tasks that align with their goals and values. By honing this skill, one can create a structured approach to daily activities, which not only enhances efficiency but also fosters a sense of accomplishment and control.

At the heart of effective time management lies the concept of prioritization. Understanding what tasks are most important and time-sensitive allows individuals to focus their efforts on activities that yield the greatest results. This is particularly crucial for young professionals and entrepreneurs who often juggle multiple responsibilities. Utilizing techniques such as the Eisenhower Matrix, which categorizes tasks based on urgency and importance, can help individuals make informed decisions about where to direct their attention. By distinguishing between what is essential and what is merely urgent, individuals can create a more strategic roadmap for their day-to-day activities, ultimately leading to better outcomes.

In addition to prioritizing tasks, establishing routines and structured schedules plays a vital role in effective time management. Routines can help reduce decision fatigue, allowing individuals to focus on executing tasks rather than constantly determining what to do next. For students, the establishment of a study schedule can enhance academic performance by ensuring that sufficient time is devoted to each subject. Similarly, for professionals and entrepreneurs, creating a daily agenda with allocated blocks for meetings, project work, and breaks can optimize mental acuity and decision-making capabilities. Consistency in routines fosters discipline, which is essential for maintaining focus and productivity.

Moreover, effective time management is intricately linked to mindfulness practices. Incorporating mindfulness techniques into one's daily schedule can help individuals become more aware of how they spend their time and where they may be prone to distractions. Mindfulness encourages a present-focused mindset, allowing individuals to engage fully in their tasks and make conscious choices about how to allocate their time. Simple practices, such as mindful breathing or short meditation sessions, can serve as powerful tools to clear the mind and enhance concentration, ultimately leading to more effective time usage.

Lastly, the interplay between time management and overall well-being cannot be overlooked. Poor time management often leads to increased stress and burnout, which can negatively impact cognitive function and performance. Conversely, when individuals manage their time effectively, they create space for self-care activities, physical exercise, and quality sleep-all of which contribute to optimal brain health. By recognizing the importance of balance and integrating time management strategies into their lives, individuals can cultivate a more fulfilling and productive lifestyle that supports their personal and professional aspirations.

Strategies to Reduce Overwhelm

Overwhelm is a common experience among young professionals, entrepreneurs, students, and individuals in various high-pressure roles. The demands of modern life can lead to a sense of chaos and an inability to focus on important tasks. To combat this, developing effective strategies to reduce overwhelm is paramount. These strategies not only help in managing stress but also enhance productivity, decision-making, and overall cognitive performance. By incorporating mindfulness techniques, structured routines, and effective time management, individuals can cultivate a mental environment conducive to success.

One of the most powerful tools in reducing overwhelm is mindfulness. Mindfulness practices, such as meditation and focused breathing, train the brain to remain present and aware, which can significantly decrease feelings of stress and anxiety. By dedicating just a few minutes each day to mindfulness exercises, individuals can foster a greater sense of control over their thoughts and emotions. This enhanced self-awareness allows for better response to stressors, ultimately leading to a more balanced approach to both personal and professional challenges.

In addition to mindfulness, establishing structured routines can greatly alleviate overwhelm. Routines provide a sense of predictability and control, which can be especially beneficial in high-stress environments. By creating a daily schedule that includes designated times for work, breaks, and personal activities, individuals can prevent the feeling of being pulled in multiple directions. This approach not only maximizes productivity but also allows for the integration of self-care practices, such as physical exercise and adequate rest, which are crucial for maintaining cognitive function and emotional well-being.

Time management is another essential strategy for combating overwhelm. Effective time management techniques, such as the Pomodoro Technique or time-blocking, encourage individuals to break tasks into manageable segments. This method not only enhances focus and concentration but also minimizes procrastination, as smaller tasks feel less daunting. Prioritizing tasks based on urgency and importance can further streamline efforts and reduce the mental clutter that contributes to feelings of overwhelm. By intentionally organizing time, individuals can create a clearer path toward achieving their goals.

Lastly, fostering emotional intelligence can play a significant role in reducing overwhelm. By developing awareness of one's emotions and understanding how to regulate them, individuals enhance their interpersonal skills and decision- making abilities. This emotional acumen allows for better communication and collaboration, reducing misunderstandings and conflicts that can lead to stress. Moreover, building emotional resilience through practices such as journaling or seeking feedback can empower individuals to navigate challenges with greater ease, ultimately contributing to a more productive and fulfilling professional and personal life.

By integrating these strategies-mindfulness practices, structured routines, effective time management, and emotional intelligence development-individuals can significantly mitigate feelings of overwhelm. These methods not only enhance cognitive capabilities but also foster a healthier mindset that supports long-term success across various domains. Embracing these approaches is essential for anyone looking to thrive in their personal and professional endeavors, paving the way for a more focused, resilient, and empowered future.

Tools for Increasing Productivity

In the pursuit of enhanced productivity, young professionals, entrepreneurs, and students alike can leverage a variety of tools designed to optimize cognitive function and foster success. One of the most powerful methods is the practice of mindfulness and meditation. These techniques not only aid in reducing stress but also sharpen focus and improve overall cognitive performance. Regular engagement in mindfulness exercises can help individuals develop greater awareness of their thoughts and emotions, enabling them to respond more effectively to challenges. By incorporating short meditation sessions into daily routines, individuals can cultivate a mindset that prioritizes clarity and presence, thus enhancing their productivity.

Another critical tool for increasing productivity is understanding and harnessing the principles of neuroplasticity. The brain's inherent ability to reorganize itself in response to learning and experience provides a unique opportunity for personal growth. Young professionals and entrepreneurs can adopt strategies that promote neuroplasticity, such as continuous learning and skill development. Engaging in new activities, whether through formal education or self-directed projects, stimulates brain pathways and fosters mental resilience. This adaptability not only enhances cognitive function but also prepares individuals to navigate the complexities of their careers with agility and innovation.

Nutrition plays a pivotal role in cognitive performance, making it essential for individuals focused on productivity to consider their dietary choices. Consuming a balanced diet rich in essential nutrients, such as omega-3 fatty acids, antioxidants, and vitamins, can significantly impact brain health. Foods like fatty fish, nuts, and leafy greens contribute to improved memory and cognitive function. Moreover, staying hydrated and minimizing processed sugars can prevent cognitive decline and maintain energy levels throughout the day, allowing individuals to remain focused and productive in their endeavors.

Physical exercise is another indispensable element in the toolkit for productivity enhancement. Research consistently shows that regular physical activity boosts brain function by increasing blood flow and stimulating the release of neurotrophic factors that promote brain health. For young professionals and athletes alike, incorporating a workout routine can lead to improved concentration, creativity, and stress management. Whether it's a brisk walk, a yoga session, or high- intensity interval training, finding a form of exercise that resonates can yield substantial benefits for both mental and physical well-being.

Lastly, the establishment of effective habits and routines is crucial for sustaining high levels of productivity. Understanding the science behind habit formation allows individuals to create actionable plans that align with their goals. Tools such as time management techniques, including the Pomodoro Technique or time blocking, can help manage workloads and reduce feelings of overwhelm. By setting clear intentions and breaking tasks into manageable segments, professionals can maintain momentum and foster a sense of accomplishment. Integrating these practices into daily life not only enhances productivity but also cultivates a proactive approach to personal and professional development, setting the stage for long-term success.

Chapter 11

The Impact of Sleep on Cognitive Function

The Science Behind Sleep and Brain Performance

The relationship between sleep and brain performance is a critical area of study that has garnered attention from researchers and professionals alike. Sleep is not merely a passive state of rest; it plays an active role in cognitive functioning, emotional regulation, and overall mental health. For young professionals, entrepreneurs, and students, understanding the science of sleep can lead to enhanced focus, improved decision-making skills, and better academic performance. The brain's performance is intricately linked to its ability to rest and rejuvenate, making the quality and quantity of sleep fundamental to achieving personal and professional goals.

During sleep, the brain engages in essential processes that consolidate memories, facilitate learning, and promote emotional well-being. Sleep cycles, particularly REM (Rapid Eye Movement) sleep, are crucial for memory consolidation. Research indicates that during REM sleep, the brain processes and stores information from the day, integrating it with existing knowledge. This process not only enhances memory retention but also supports creativity and problem-solving abilities. For young professionals and entrepreneurs, a well- rested brain is better equipped to tackle complex challenges, innovate, and make strategic decisions.

Moreover, sleep deprivation can have profound effects on cognitive function. Lack of adequate sleep is associated with diminished attention span, impaired judgment, and decreased problem-solving skills. In high-stakes environments, such as in the world of business or academia, these deficits can lead to significant setbacks. Young professionals and executives must prioritize sleep hygiene to combat these risks. Simple practices, such as establishing a consistent sleep schedule, creating a restful environment, and minimizing screen time before bed, can dramatically improve sleep quality and, consequently, cognitive performance.

The interplay between sleep and emotional intelligence is another vital aspect to consider. Quality sleep contributes to emotional regulation, allowing individuals to respond to stressors with a clearer mindset. For entrepreneurs and managers who frequently navigate high-pressure situations, maintaining emotional intelligence is essential for effective leadership. By ensuring adequate rest, professionals can enhance their ability to connect with others, make informed decisions, and foster a positive work environment. Thus, optimizing sleep is not only about cognitive enhancement but also about cultivating healthier interpersonal relationships.

In conclusion, the science behind sleep and brain performance underscores the importance of prioritizing rest in our daily routines. For young professionals, students, and anyone seeking to optimize their cognitive abilities, embracing healthy sleep habits can lead to substantial gains in focus, creativity, and emotional intelligence. By understanding how sleep affects brain function, individuals can harness the power of rest to enhance their overall performance, paving the way for greater success in their personal and professional lives. As we delve deeper into the various facets of brain optimization, recognizing sleep as a foundational element will be integral to our journey toward peak performance.

Strategies for Improving Sleep Hygiene

Sleep hygiene is a crucial factor in optimizing cognitive function and overall productivity, especially for young professionals, entrepreneurs, and students. The quality of sleep directly influences our mental acuity, emotional regulation, and decision-making abilities. By adopting effective sleep hygiene practices, individuals can significantly enhance their focus and performance, paving the way for personal and professional success. This subchapter will explore various strategies designed to improve sleep hygiene, ensuring that readers can harness the restorative power of sleep to support their ambitions.

One of the most effective strategies for improving sleep hygiene is establishing a consistent sleep schedule. Going to bed and waking up at the same time every day helps regulate the body's internal clock, making it easier to fall asleep and wake up refreshed. This consistency reinforces the natural sleep-wake cycle, which is particularly beneficial for those who juggle multiple responsibilities, such as work, studies, and personal projects. Additionally, creating a relaxing bedtime routine-such as reading, meditating, or taking a warm bath-can signal to the body that it is time to wind down, further promoting the transition into sleep.

The sleep environment plays a significant role in sleep quality. To create an optimal setting for rest, it is essential to minimize noise, light, and other distractions. Young professionals and entrepreneurs often find themselves working late into the night, which can lead to a chaotic and overstimulating environment. Implementing strategies like blackout curtains, white noise machines, or comfortable bedding can enhance the quality of sleep. Furthermore, keeping the bedroom reserved solely for sleep and intimacy helps to psychologically associate the space with relaxation and rest, making it easier to unwind at the end of the day.

Mindfulness and relaxation techniques can also contribute to better sleep hygiene. Practices such as meditation, deep breathing exercises, or progressive muscle relaxation can reduce stress and anxiety, which are common barriers to restful sleep. Young professionals and students, in particular, may experience heightened stress due to academic and career pressures. By incorporating mindfulness practices into their nightly routine, individuals can cultivate a sense of calm that allows for a smoother transition into sleep. Additionally, these techniques can improve emotional resilience and clarity, which are essential for effective decision-making and relationship-building.

Nutrition and physical activity are intertwined with sleep quality, making them critical components of sleep hygiene. Consuming a balanced diet rich in nutrients can support brain health and overall well-being, influencing sleep patterns positively. Foods high in magnesium, such as leafy greens and nuts, as well as those rich in tryptophan, like turkey and dairy, can encourage better sleep. Furthermore, regular physical activity has been shown to promote deeper sleep and enhance mood. Young professionals and entrepreneurs should aim to incorporate exercise into their daily routine, not only for physical health but also for its profound impact on cognitive function and sleep quality.

In conclusion, improving sleep hygiene is vital for anyone looking to enhance their cognitive abilities and achieve personal goals. By adopting strategies such as maintaining a consistent sleep schedule, creating an optimal sleep environment, practicing mindfulness techniques, and paying attention to nutrition and exercise, individuals can significantly improve their sleep quality. This, in turn, fosters better mental acuity, focus, and resilience, enabling young professionals, entrepreneurs, and students to navigate their challenges more effectively and reach their full potential. Prioritizing sleep is not merely a matter of health; it is an investment in success.

The Role of Rest in Achieving Success

Rest plays a pivotal role in achieving success, particularly in the fast-paced environment that young professionals, entrepreneurs, students, and leaders often navigate. While the hustle culture promotes non-stop productivity as a hallmark of success, research increasingly highlights the importance of adequate rest for optimal cognitive function and overall well-being. Just as physical exercise strengthens the body, rest rejuvenates the mind, allowing individuals to perform at their best. Acknowledging this relationship between rest and success is the first step toward fostering habits that enhance focus, creativity, and resilience.

The science of sleep is deeply intertwined with cognitive performance. Quality sleep enhances memory consolidation, emotional regulation, and problem-solving abilities, which are crucial for decision-making in both academic and professional settings. During sleep, the brain undergoes various restorative processes, including the clearance of toxins and the reorganization of neural connections. For students preparing for exams or professionals facing critical projects, prioritizing sleep can lead to improved retention and recall of information, ultimately influencing academic and career outcomes. By understanding that rest is not a luxury but a necessity, individuals can better align their habits with their goals.

Additionally, mindfulness techniques, such as meditation and deep breathing exercises, can significantly influence how effectively one utilizes rest. These practices promote relaxation and mental clarity, allowing individuals to recharge their cognitive resources. Engaging in mindfulness helps cultivate a state of awareness that reduces stress and fosters a sense of calm, which can enhance focus and productivity. This is particularly relevant for entrepreneurs and executives who often bear the weight of high-stakes decisions. Incorporating brief mindfulness sessions throughout the day can serve as a restorative break, leading to sharper thinking and improved emotional intelligence.

Physical activity also complements the role of rest in achieving success. Exercise has been shown to boost mood and cognitive function, creating a synergy between physical and mental well-being. Regular engagement in physical activity can improve sleep quality, making it easier for individuals to reap the benefits of restorative rest. For athletes, in particular, understanding the balance between training and recovery is essential for peak performance. By integrating structured rest periods with physical training routines, athletes can maximize their potential while minimizing the risk of burnout and injury.

Ultimately, cultivating a mindset that values rest as an integral part of success is crucial for anyone striving for personal and professional growth. By establishing routines that prioritize both work and rest, individuals can enhance their cognitive abilities, emotional intelligence, and overall productivity. A holistic approach that incorporates sufficient rest, mindfulness practices, and physical activity can lead to sustainable success and resilience in the face of challenges. Embracing the power of rest is not just a strategy for short-term gains; it is a foundational element of long-term achievement and fulfillment.

Chapter 12

Conclusion: Integrating Focus and Mindfulness into Daily Life

Creating a Personal Action Plan

Creating a Personal Action Plan is an essential step for young professionals, entrepreneurs, students, and anyone looking to enhance their cognitive capabilities and achieve personal goals. This plan serves as a roadmap, guiding individuals through the process of honing their mental acuity and focus while incorporating mindfulness techniques. It is imperative to understand that a successful action plan is not a one-size-fits-all approach but should be tailored to meet individual needs, aspirations, and circumstances. By addressing various aspects such as goal setting, mindfulness practices, and lifestyle choices, this plan can significantly enhance one's ability to perform at their best.

The first step in creating a Personal Action Plan is to define clear, actionable goals. Utilizing Cognitive Behavioral Therapy (CBT) principles can be particularly effective in this regard. Start by identifying specific areas for improvement, whether they relate to personal development, academic success, or professional growth. Break these goals down into smaller, manageable tasks that can be tracked over time. This approach not only makes the objectives feel less overwhelming but also provides opportunities for celebrating small wins, which can enhance motivation and sustain engagement.

Incorporating mindfulness and meditation practices into your daily routine is crucial for enhancing focus and reducing stress. Mindfulness techniques encourage individuals to stay present, which can improve decision-making and cognitive performance. Set aside dedicated time each day for mindfulness exercises, whether through meditation, deep breathing, or simply taking a moment to reflect in silence. These practices can help clear mental clutter, allowing for greater clarity and a more profound connection to one's goals. By integrating mindfulness into your Personal Action Plan, you create a buffer against the distractions and pressures that often accompany a busy lifestyle.

Nutrition and physical exercise are vital components that significantly impact cognitive function. As you draft your Personal Action Plan, consider incorporating strategies to optimize your diet for brain health. This includes prioritizing whole foods rich in antioxidants, healthy fats, and essential nutrients that promote cognitive clarity. Additionally, regular physical activity has been shown to enhance brain function by improving blood flow and stimulating the release of beneficial neurotransmitters. Design a balanced routine that includes both mental and physical exercises, ensuring that you are nurturing your body and mind simultaneously.

Finally, the significance of sleep cannot be overlooked in a Personal Action Plan aimed at improving cognitive performance. Quality sleep is foundational for memory retention, emotional regulation, and overall brain health. Establishing a consistent sleep schedule, creating a restful environment, and practicing good sleep hygiene are all essential strategies to improve sleep quality. By ensuring that your body is well-rested, you lay the groundwork for optimal cognitive function and productivity. As you implement your Personal Action Plan, remember that it is a dynamic document that can evolve as you grow, learn, and adapt to new challenges and opportunities.

Sustaining focus and Mindfulness for Long-Term Success

Sustaining focus and mindfulness is crucial for long-term success in both personal and professional settings. As young professionals and aspiring entrepreneurs navigate the complexities of their careers, developing habits that promote sustained attention and clarity can make a significant difference. Mindfulness techniques, in particular, offer powerful tools for enhancing cognitive function and emotional regulation, enabling individuals to remain engaged and productive even amidst distractions and stress. By integrating mindfulness practices into their daily routines, individuals can cultivate a resilient mindset that not only supports immediate goals but also fosters a sustainable path toward achievement.

One of the foundational concepts in maintaining focus is the understanding of neuroplasticity-the brain's remarkable ability to reorganize itself through experience. By harnessing this capability, individuals can train their brains to prioritize focus and mindfulness. Techniques such as visualization, positive affirmations, and deliberate practice can reshape neural pathways, reinforcing the mental habits necessary for success. For young professionals and entrepreneurs, this means that by consistently engaging in activities that promote concentration and awareness, they can enhance their cognitive agility and decision-making skills, ultimately leading to improved performance in their respective fields.

Mindfulness and meditation practices serve as vital components in sustaining focus. These techniques not only help in reducing stress but also enhance cognitive functions such as memory and attention span. Simple practices like mindful breathing, body scans, and guided meditation can be easily incorporated into daily life, allowing individuals to reset their mental state and improve their ability to concentrate on tasks at hand. For students, in particular, these practices can optimize brain function during study sessions and exam preparation, while executives and managers can benefit from mindfulness in high-pressure situations to make clearer, more strategic decisions.

Additionally, the role of nutrition in cognitive performance cannot be overlooked when discussing sustained focus. A balanced diet rich in nutrients that support brain health-such as omega-3 fatty acids, antioxidants, and vitamins—can significantly impact mental clarity and energy levels. Young professionals and entrepreneurs should prioritize nutrition as part of their overall strategy for enhancing cognitive abilities. By understanding how food choices influence brain function, individuals can optimize their diets to support sustained focus and maintain high productivity levels throughout the day.

Finally, establishing productive habits and routines is essential for maintaining focus over the long term. The science of habits reveals that small, consistent actions can lead to significant changes in behavior. Young professionals and students alike can benefit from developing structured schedules that prioritize tasks, incorporate breaks, and allow for periods of reflection. Coupled with effective time management strategies, these routines can reduce feelings of overwhelm and promote a more focused approach to both academic and professional challenges. By committing to these practices, individuals can create an environment conducive to sustained mindfulness and focus, ultimately paving the way for enduring success.

Encouragement for Ongoing Growth and Development

In the journey toward personal and professional success, ongoing growth and development serve as essential pillars. For young professionals, entrepreneurs, and students, cultivating a mindset oriented toward continuous improvement can significantly enhance both cognitive abilities and overall performance. This chapter emphasizes the importance of nurturing a growth-oriented perspective, encouraging readers to embrace challenges, learn from setbacks, and seek out opportunities for development. By fostering a mindset that values progress over perfection, individuals can unlock their potential and build habits that support lifelong learning.

One of the key components of ongoing growth is understanding neuroplasticity, the brain's remarkable ability to reorganize itself and form new connections throughout life. By harnessing this capability, individuals can actively train their brains to improve performance and resilience. Engaging in activities that challenge cognitive functions-such as learning a new language, solving complex problems, or practicing mindfulness-can stimulate neural pathways and enhance mental acuity. This dynamic approach to brain training not only fosters intellectual growth but also promotes adaptability, a crucial trait for navigating the ever-evolving landscape of modern careers.

Mindfulness and meditation practices are powerful tools for fostering ongoing development, particularly for those in high-pressure environments. Through regular mindfulness exercises, individuals can enhance focus, reduce stress, and improve cognitive function. Techniques such as deep breathing, guided visualization, and mindful observation can create a mental space conducive to reflection and self-improvement. By incorporating these practices into daily routines, professionals can develop greater emotional intelligence, sharpen decision-making abilities, and cultivate a balanced approach to both work and personal life.

Nutritional choices also play a critical role in cognitive performance and overall mental well- being. Understanding the impact of diet on brain health is vital for anyone seeking to optimize their cognitive abilities. Consuming a balanced diet rich in antioxidants, healthy fats, vitamins, and minerals can support brain function and enhance memory retention. Furthermore, staying adequately hydrated and avoiding excessive caffeine or sugar can help maintain focus and clarity throughout the day. By prioritizing nutrition, individuals can create a foundation for sustained cognitive excellence and improved productivity.

Finally, the establishment of effective habits and routines is essential for fostering ongoing growth. Understanding the science of habits helps individuals create actionable plans that align with their goals. Additionally, effective time management strategies can significantly reduce feelings of overwhelm, allowing for focused work periods that enhance cognitive function. Coupled with quality sleep, regular physical activity, and emotional regulation techniques, these practices form a comprehensive approach to personal development. By committing to ongoing growth and development, individuals empower themselves to navigate the complexities of their careers and personal lives with confidence and resilience.